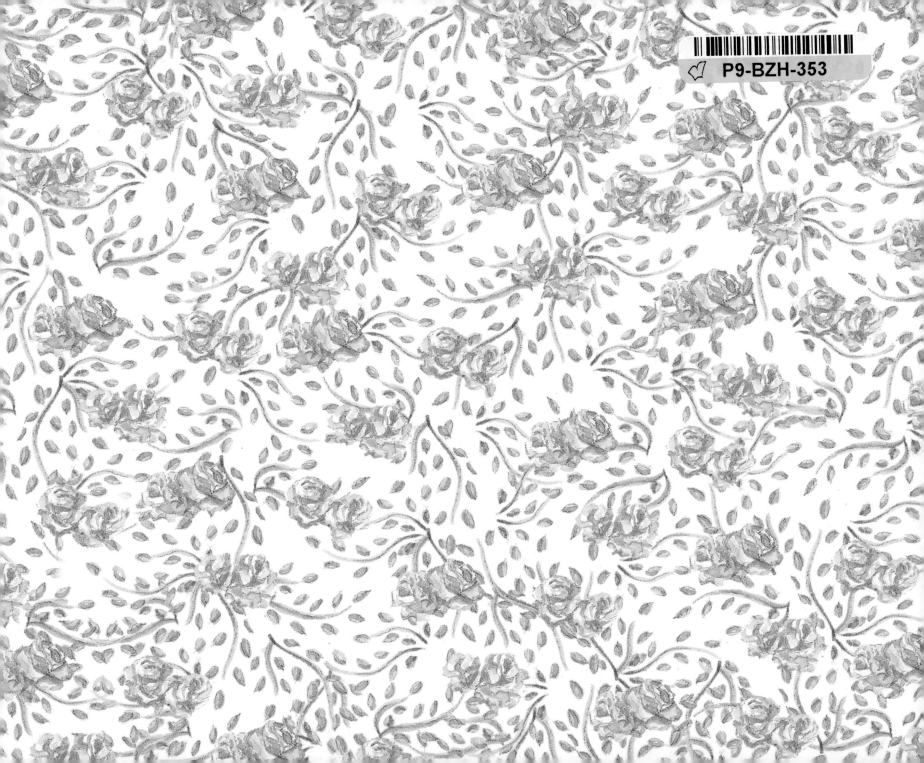

P9-BZH-353

Presented to...

_____

With love ...

_____

on

_____

God's Wisdom for Little Girls

Elizabeth George

Paintings by Judy Luenebrink

HARVEST HOUSE PUBLISHERS
EUGENE, OREGON

God's Wisdom for Little Girls
Text copyright © 2000 by Elizabeth George
Illustrations copyright © 2000 by Judy Luenebrink
Published by Harvest House Publishers
Eugene, OR 97402

Library of Congress Cataloging-in-Publication Data
George, Elizabeth, 1944–
    God's wisdom for little girls / Elizabeth George; paintings by Judy Luenebrink.
      p. cm.
    Summary: The author interprets parts of the book of Proverbs for very young girls.
    ISBN 0-7369-0427-1
    1. Girls—Christian life—Juvenile literature. 2. Bible. O.T. Proverbs XXXI
10-31—Juvenile literature. [1. Christian life.] I. Luenebrink, Judy, ill. II. Title.
BV4551.2 .G46 2000
248.8'2—dc21
                                        00-024331

For more information regarding the author and artist of this book, please contact:

Elizabeth George
P.O. Box 2879
Belfair, WA 98528
www.ElizabethGeorge.com

Judy Luenebrink
judyluenebrink@sbcglobal.net

Design and production by Matthew Shoemaker

Unless otherwise indicated, Scripture quotations are from *The International Children's Bible, New Century Version,* copyright © 1986 by Word Publishing, Nashville, Tennessee. Used by permission.

Scripture quotations marked KJV are from the King James Version of the Bible.

Printed in China.

16 17 18 / LP / 36 35 34

For Taylor Jane Zaengle

These verses and this book are written for you out of a heart of love.
Happy first birthday, dear little granddaughter!

Dear Friend,

   What you hold in your hands is a part of my heart—a book written for girls about the qualities and traits that God exalts in Proverbs 31:10-31. It's true that this passage from the Bible describes the character of a woman who loves God. Yet as one of those women who are instilling God's Word and God's ways into the next generation, you can pass these qualities on to the very young. You see, the qualities never change—just our age and our arena!

   It is my prayer that you and the little girls in your life will enjoy sharing this book together. I pray that you will enjoy each character quality (they are named for clarity), each rhyme (they focus on the actions that make up the daily life of a little girl), and, of course, each charming and beautiful painting by artist Judy Luenebrink. I only wish I had written this book when my two daughters were growing up!

   In His wonderful love,

   Elizabeth George

Once upon a time, very long ago,
God penned a poem so every girl could grow.
Would you like to be wise? Do you want to be kind?
Then come on and hear what God has in mind.

Snuggle up close, get cozy and see
A girl just like you—as sweet as can be.
Let's read a few rhymes and look at some pictures
Of God's little girl as seen through the Scriptures.

God's Little Girl Is... Priceless

"A virtuous woman, who can find?"
So begins this rhyme of mine,
"Worth more than rubies," so we're told.
God's little girl is better than gold!

❧

Who can find a virtuous woman?
For her price is far above rubies.
PROVERBS 31:10 KJV

God's Little Girl Is...
Kind

Being good to others is so hard to do!
But this is exactly what God asks of you.
So do what you can to be kind to others,
And that includes your sisters and brothers!

❧

Her husband trusts her completely.
With her, he has everything he needs.
She does him good and not harm
for as long as she lives.
PROVERBS 31:11,12

God's Little Girl Is... Eager

As "busy as a bee," a real "eager beaver,"
That's how God sees His little weaver.
She's ready, she's set, she can't wait to start—
She always works hard with a song in her heart.

❦

She looks for wool and linen.

She likes to work with her hands.

PROVERBS 31:13

God's Little Girl Is...

Helpful

God's little girl goes with Mom to the store.
(Oh, how they love to shop and explore!)
And when they get home she helps Mom prepare
Food for the family to show how they care.

❦

She is like a trader's ship. She goes far to get food.
PROVERBS 31:14

God's Little Girl Is...

Cheerful

What's that I hear? That loud cock-a-doo?
It's time to get up—taste the day while it's new!
But first praise the Lord, say a verse and a prayer:
"Love one another," and "God, help me to care."

❧

She gets up while it is still dark.
She prepares food for her family.

PROVERBS 31:15

God's Little Girl Is...
Busy

The garden of God's little girl—how grand!
It began with a dream, a prayer, and a plan.
Nothing this splendid just happens, we know:
It takes time and care for flowers to grow.

❧

She looks at a field and buys it.
With money she has earned,
she plants a vineyard.

PROVERBS 31:16

God's Little Girl Is...
Hearty

"Buckle your shoe!" Do you know this rhyme?
"Ready, set, go!" It helps every time.
To give it our all, at school, home, and play,
"I need Your strength, dear Lord," we pray.

❦

She does her work with energy.

Her arms are strong.

PROVERBS 31:17

God's Little Girl Is...

Diligent

Can you think of something that gives you delight?
That makes you feel good in your bed at night?
That brings you a feeling compared to none?
The pleasure of knowing a job's been well done!

❧

She makes sure that what she makes is good. She works
by her lamp late into the night. She makes thread
with her hands and weaves her own cloth.
PROVERBS 31:18,19

	Mon	Tues	Wed
Smile	★		
Make Bed	★		
Brush Teeth	★		
Set Table	★		
Feed Cat	★		

God's Little Girl Is... Caring

"Oh, Mommy, look—see who's passing by!"
(God's little girl looks ready to cry.)
Her sweet heart is breaking for someone in need.
"Lord, let me help them and do a kind deed."

She welcomes the poor. She helps the needy.
PROVERBS 31:20

God's Little Girl Is... Prepared

Some fear the winter—the snow, sleet, and rain.
Not God's little girl. (Please, let me explain.)
Her warm, woolly coat is ready in advance,
God's girl is all set for each circumstance.

❧

She does not worry
about her family when it snows.
PROVERBS 31:21

God's Little Girl Is...
Creative

A keen eye for beauty has God's little girl,
She gets it from looking at God's pretty world.
His handiwork, everywhere, and the sky throughout
Teaches His splendor as she looks about.

She makes coverings for her bed.
Her clothes are made of linen
and other expensive material.

PROVERBS 31:22

God's Little Girl Is...
Prayerful

"I'm not married yet," God's little girl muses.
"Someday it might happen, if that's what God chooses!
I pray he'll be wise and someone who's nice—
A man who loves family and gives good advice."

Her husband is recognized at the city meetings.
He makes decisions as one of the leaders of the land.

PROVERBS 31:23

God's Little Girl Is...

Artistic

"What else do I dream? Would you like to know?
To make pretty things—just like a real pro.
Will I paint? Will I sew? How will I create?
I don't know just yet, but I'll try as I wait!"

She makes linen clothes and sells them.
She provides belts to the merchants.

PROVERBS 31:24

God's Little Girl Is...

Confident

What is true happiness? What makes you smile?
It's knowing all's well when facing a trial.
It's doing the best you can do every day,
Then trusting the Lord to protect all the way.

She is strong and respected by the people.

She looks forward to the future with joy.

Proverbs 31:25

God's Little Girl Is...

Gracious

Some folks hurt others by "speaking their mind."
But God's girl speaks wisdom—only says what is kind.
She calms a hurt soul and heals a sad heart
By saying kind words instead of what's "smart."

❧

She speaks wise words.
And she teaches others to be kind.
PROVERBS 31:26

God's Little Girl Is...
Careful

To take care of people is how home is run;
It takes spunk and vigor and getting things done.
You pray for your family and watch how they fare;
You look out for others with kind, loving care.

❧

She watches over her family.
And she is always busy.

PROVERBS 31:27

God's Little Girl Is...

Thoughtful

"I love you, dear Mom—and I want you to know it.
Each day I ask God to please help me show it!
And if, when I'm grown, I have little ones too,
I pray that I'll be a mom…just like you!"

❧

Her children bless her. Her husband also praises her.
He says, "There are many excellent wives,
but you are better than all of them."

PROVERBS 31:28,29

God's Little Girl Is...

God's Child

Do you want to be pretty? A fine piece of art?
Even better than "pretty" is Jesus in your heart.
If you love Him the most and follow His ways,
His beauty inside you will reap His best praise.

❧

Charm can fool you, and beauty can trick you.
But a woman who respects the Lord should be praised.
Proverbs 31:30

God's Little Girl Is...

Cherished

"A virtuous woman, who can find?"
So began this rhyme of mine,
But now that it's over it's plain to see
Just what God wants His girl to be.

"Lord, help me to grow from a girl to a lady,
To blossom and bloom into all that I may be.
As I learn and grow, and I do what You say,
May this little girl be Your woman some day!"

❧

Give her the reward she has earned.
She should be openly praised for what she has done.
PROVERBS 31:31

Words to Know

The Word	What It Means	Where You'll Find It
Scriptures	The Holy Bible, God's Word	introduction
virtuous	good and godly	verses 10 and 31
hearty	eager and with energy	verse 17
diligent	hard working	verses 18 and 19
circumstance	event	verse 21
creative	use of imagination	verse 22
keen	sharp, aware	verse 22
muses	thinks about	verse 23
artistic	a skillful expert	verse 24
confident	sure	verse 25
gracious	kind and polite	verse 26
wisdom	good judgment	verse 26
godly	good and God-loving	verses 28 and 29
charm	smooth talk	verse 30
cherished	loved and adored	verse 31